The Fragrant Soil

Dr. Om Prakash Yadava

DEDICATION

This work is dedicated to my wife Mrs.Kanti Yadava who took me to Varanasi and showed me a glimpse of life and values of that city and who endlessly remained in quest of happiness and kept me involved in her quest.

CONTENTS

ACKNOWLEDGMENTS

Author has received inspiration from a host of lives dedicated in search of happiness through limitless material gains and also those who saw every happiness available within their means and that has inspired this work and obviously he stands indebted to all those lives.

PROLOGUE

It was the hot summer of end May month. Outside temperature was ranging from forty six degree Celsius to forty eight degree Celsius and the hot blazing sun was emitting & radiating scorching heat all around. The mid-day had fast approached and the general compartment of the train had become like a hot oven. Wherever, he could put his hands, legs or eyes it was hot and hot only. The compartment was jam packed with human bodies & heads ranging from young children to old men & women, all drenched in sweat and the foul stench of sweat soaked in their dirty clothes having filled the whole compartment was so repulsive that bearing it was a ghastly act but he had no other option. Though a pair of small ceiling fans fitted with guards were hanging from the ceiling of the compartment but they were not functioning. Some passengers had tried to play with the switches but nothing moved.

As long as the train moved things were within manageable limits as the gush of hot wind coming from outside through the open windows would sweep away the stench and dry the sweat; but whenever train halted at a station it was really horrible to withstand the stench and over and above there was not even an inch of space available to stretch legs or hands or relax.

He had boarded the Varanasi bound train at Nasik Road station in the morning around eight hours when heat was not much. Jumping over men & women he had entered the compartment through a window. In fact some of his friends had lifted him & pushed him inside the compartment as the entry gates were crammed with men hanging on foot board holding the iron bars. As long as the train had halted at that station he could not find space to place his foot down and was practically swinging over the heads & bodies of the crowd, holding in his hands a bag containing his clothing & other essential items. In the melee he could not find even opportunity to bid good bye to his friends who had come to see him off and had helped him enter the compartment.

As the train moved, gradually crowd settled down and he got some space to stand up on his own and after an hour he managed some space on the floor to sit down in the gantry. The train halted at all major stations en route and he observed the repetition of same story what he had found at his boarding station, people fighting and entering the compartment passing over the heads and bodies of passengers already present in the compartment.

After the train had passed Bhusawal junction when the heat was at its peak, he suddenly noticed that an old man wearing dirty clothes who was sitting very tight in a corner near toilet became restive and started vomiting. The area around him became dirty and all those sitting there started abusing him but no body came for his help. He fainted after sometimes and fell on the floor. He wanted to help him but situation was so tight that reaching that place was not easy and also he feared losing the place where he himself was sitting.

Two hours later train reached Khandwa station where some sweepers came who lifted that man down the train and just brushed the dirty area. Sitting so tight in the same posture, experiencing the horrendous situation at every station and traveling over several hours he reached Itarsi junction.

Evening had knocked at the doors and the heat of blazing sun had faded away but still the compartment was full of heat & humidity and his body had become stiff of being in a tight situation for several hours. A number of passengers were getting down for taking water and eatables from the platform and some had completed their journey and were alighting with their belongings. Suddenly he noticed that a person who was sleeping on a top berth for several hours was getting down with the bag which he had been using as a pillow keeping below his head.

Before anyone else could notice that, he immediately got up, rushed hurriedly and practically jumped up to occupy that seat cum berth; opened his bag, took out a long cloth looking like a towel and spread that over the berth. He then felt a little relaxed and comfortable for the rest of his journey which was still over fifteen hours ahead. He knew that there were many old men & women sitting below in uncomfortable situation but he did not mind for them though in normal conditions he might have taken care of them.

After a little rest he came down and looked outside the window and saw a tea vendor passing by on the platform. He called him and purchased tea which was contained in a small paper cup. It was costing very high but as he sipped the tea he found that the taste & quality was poor except that the same was hot. He started murmuring & rebuking the tea vendor for looting the passengers with such a bad quality of tea. One passenger who noticed him unhappy with the tea simply spoke & cautioned him that,

"Itarsi is the biggest railway junction of India where trains arrive from all the directions and corners of the country and depart to them. All sorts of wrong people assemble here and all types of wrong activities go on here and organized gangs operate them. If any passenger is not careful he can be robbed off & looted of all that he has and these robbers are using many types of methods. Better be careful and don't come in trap of vendors moving on the platform and don't accept anything from anyone."

He simply nodded to the advice and became careful. He knew that train would be halting there for about half an hour and he was feeling like easing himself but he preferred to stick to his berth and take care of the bag that he had. When the train moved and the commotion & bustle of the platform disappeared then he came down and decided to go to the toilet to ease himself. The entire gallery was full of passengers and with a lot of difficulty he could reach the toilet which was very dirty & foul smelling but he had no choice but to use that. The train was moving in its usual mood even halting at unspecified places in addition to stopping at specified stations. Around nine thirty in the night it reached some big station. He requested the passenger sitting just below his berth to take care of his bag & seat and got down and looked out through window and found that station to be Jabalpur. He alighted from the compartment and purchased some eatables & drinking water from a railway stall, came back to his berth and took them.

He had heard about Jabalpur for beautiful cliffs of river Narmada and writers of Hindi literature and also to be notorious for secret gangs of THUGS which British Colonel William Henry Sleeman had eradicated but he never had opportunity to visit those cliffs. Once the train left that station, he stretched himself on the berth and slept.

There was a great commotion and many types of sounds were audible that woke him up. He looked this way and that way but could not find anything abnormal though it looked as a clear morning. He asked one of his fellow passenger as to what was causing the noise.

"It is Naini Railway station just before Allahabad junction and a herd of Pandas are disturbing every passenger and despite our clear telling that we are not pilgrims & we have no interest in taking bath at the Sangam still they are disturbing us. Though GRP (general railway police) personnel are visible standing on the platform but no one is there to question them and those goons are freely troubling the passengers." He was taken aback to see that the gateway to the holiest city of India was having the most unholy situation which shook him terribly and he was in a dilemma that whether he would be successful to find

what he had set out himself in search of, in another holy city of India- Varansi, which was just one hundred and odd kilometers away. But having hope against the odds he decided to continue with his journey. As the train was passing over river Yamuna bridge he was touched by a serene breeze and a divine sight of majestic river which is considered as the daughter of Lord Sun & younger sister of Lord Yama-the god of death, full of clear green waters which made him forget the bad experience he had just a few minutes back. He saw some people throwing coins in the river water below, the significance of which he could not understand. However, to his query one co-passenger told him that to be a pious act and people do that while making some prayers to the holy river. The sound of vibrating & rattling iron structure of the double-storied bridge, constructed over the normal traffic road down below; though loud had created a feel of celestial music, which momentarily took him away from the world of pleasures & pains. However, that lasted only for five minutes and the train crossed the bridge.

Moving slowly with occasional halts, the train reached Allahabad Junction which though very big in expanse did not show any sign either of holiness for which Tirthraj Prayag was known and attracts lakhs & lakhs of pilgrims every year, nor of the magnanimity of Pandit Nehru who was founder & architect of the place. Rather the platforms looked very dirty and full of nuisance and crowd. Train halted at Allahabad junction for a very long period of time and therefrom it moved at snail's pace halting very frequently due to unauthorized chain pulling by wayside passengers & students and because of signals not being available to go ahead.

By the time train reached Varanasi Cantt station it was afternoon with sun lowering down on the western horizon and losing its heat and radiation effect. This was the terminal station - the end of the journey of train. Along with all other passengers he also alighted at the magnificent but very dirty Varanasi Cantonment station and being pushed along with the outgoing crowd came out of the station without knowing where had he to go therefrom. He found many cycle-rickshaw pullers coaxing and cajoling him for taking him to this place or that place or wherever he wanted to go but he humbly avoided them and slowly moved down to the main road. However, he himself did not know where he wanted to go but still he moved as a pedestrian, in the direction the road was leading into the main city.

****

CHAPTER I

The Search

*T*hough the day had been very hot and uncomfortable with hot wind blowing through out the day forcing people to move on the roads with their heads & faces covered with caps & cloths, but the evening was quite pleasant.

Sitting at the banks of the great river Ganges, watching the vast expanse of pious waters and its endless elegant & subtle flow towards eternity, Rajesh Khobragade was having so many thoughts divine and emancipating passing through his mind. The first thought that came to his mind was that of Lord Rama who had blessed & emancipated so many sinners and had lived his whole life for the establishment of DHARMA - the righteousness and had also suffered the endless pangs of pains. Though He is treated by Hindus as an incarnation of Lord Vishnu from the feet of whom the mighty river flowing in front of him had originated, yet he had to request a boatsman to help him cross that river when he was going to exile along with his wife Sita & younger brother Laxman, accepting the orders of his father King Dashrath.

He pondered and pondered over and felt that if the human embodiment of supreme deity had to undergo such a situation then what could be the fate of normal human beings like him and therefore what all he had experienced in his life so far, was nothing significant & obviously negligible but immediately another thought flashed to his mind that, whatever, Lord Rama did and the sufferings & pains he underwent were meant for some purpose, some useful purpose for the noble people of the world and lessons for posterity; but what was he doing, was there any purpose behind his doings? No sooner that thought came to him, he could realize that he had come to that city in search of something but what was that was yet unknown & unidentified to him.

He remembered the horrors of his journey from Nasik Road to Varanasi and how the people in distress became so selfish & so self-centered that they forgot even the least of human considerations, concern and sympathy to others. What a world and its unwritten ethics?

But he felt happy of having travelled in the general compartment of a train of the Indian railways which gave him a glimpse of the realities of life a common man faces in the train journey which otherwise he would not have tasted elsewhere, that how normal Indians were heartless to their own fellow men & how were they treated like fodder & hay by the ruling system even in the twenty first century.

He also remembered that how had he reached up to the banks of the river Ganges. In fact on that very day after alighting from the train and having come out to the main road, as he was moving and going ahead aimlessly that he thought of going to some Lord Hanuman(monkey god) temple as that day was a Tuesday. He asked someone on the road for the directions, who advised him to take a cycle rickshaw and go to the famous SANKAT MOCHAN temple which was a few kilometers away and he followed the advice received.

The temple was originally located in a solitary place but the vast expanse of city and its population had brought it in the midst of the human inhabitation and the jungle of concrete all around.

On the way rickshaw puller who was in late fifties liked to have some discussions with him as was the usual practice of Varanasi people. Accordingly he was telling so many things about himself, about the city, its culture and life in his Bhojpuri language which Rajesh was not able to follow much and was simply replying in yes or no or simply nodding his head.

The long discussion made rickshaw puller guess that he was some outsider and might be, had come on pilgrimage as the city was having half of its population as floating consisting of outsiders having come on pilgrimage and also foreigners to see the city, its temples and Sarnath- the Buddhist Vihar where Lord Buddha had given first sermons after attaining enlightenment to his five disciples.

On reaching the temple rickshaw puller asked him to get down, charged the reasonable amount of fair and showed him the pathway how to reach the temple.

Rajesh knew that temple had been a target of terrorist attacks in the past and was still in their hit list. The devotees were coming, having quick darshan of the deity and going away. They were not sitting in the temple precincts and hardly a couple of persons were seen sitting in the Mandpam (covered area in front of the deity).

He went to the sanctum, had darshan, came out and sat in the Mandpam. He was able to see the deity very clearly and continued looking at it for long, as looking at the deity gave him a peaceful & relaxed feeling. After a couple of hours the arrival of devotees stopped and the temple activities also stopped. A priest came out of the sanctum and finding him alone sitting there asked him if he wanted some help.

He told the priest of his coming from the far off place in Maharastra state and requested for some place where he could stay for some days. Priest advised him to go to nearby Dharmashala (an inn run by some religious organization where pilgrims could stay on payment of nominal fee) and tell the name of the priest as reference.

The stay was arranged and he was reasonably comfortable, mixing with pilgrims coming from Maharastra and other western parts of India and moving with them, going to various places and taking part in religious activities. He was able to get food in some or the other Bhandara or Langars (religious feeding of pilgrims arranged by temples, individuals and organizations) and was happily spending his days but the amount of money whatever he had carried with him was gradually reducing which was worrying him and still he was not able to find as to what was he searching for.

His Dharmashala was very close to Tulasi Manas Mandir where every evening there used to be religious congregations and lectures by eminent speakers on various subjects mostly related to religion, ethics and theology. One evening he reluctantly went there to attend the lecture, however, found the discourse quite engrossing & illuminating and thereafter he made it a point to go there often & on and listen to the words & thoughts of the speakers. One day one speaker was explaining the life and actions of Lord Rama and was making a lot of references from the holy literatures, however, the essence of lecture what he could understand was that,

"Let us not consider Rama as an incarnation of supreme deity as that is a hypothetical assumption, however, fact remains that he was a prince-son of a king and obviously a human being but the exceptional and extra

*ordinary virtues that he possessed & sacrifices that he made have placed him close to supreme deity and the world feels delighted to call him as MARYADA PURUSHOTTAM- an **idol of ideals.** He had a mission, a vision, a purpose, an objective and on top of them a selfless life. He not only set the highest standards of obeying his father even for the most undesirable demand but denounced the throne which was going to be his.*

Even while en route to exile and while dwelling in forests he maintained the highest standards of life. He was the true friend of the friends and destroyer of sinners & the devils who came on the path of righteousness. He had the treasure, the endless wealth of virtues or in fact he was rather the embodiment of wealth of virtues."

The essence of the discourse enabled Rajesh Khobragade to identify that he was in search of some wealth which could make his life happy & worth living but what that wealth was, was still a far cry and beyond his comprehension. That sparked a ray of hope in him that someday he would be able to find out that wealth, but when and how? that was still hidden in the womb of time.

"Swamy ji! You have explained many things of religion, its tenets and duties but I am not able to understand everything though I had been very attentively listening to what all you said. Many things I may pick up gradually in form of some thread but please let me understand what is my duty as a normal human being."

"Though a very elaborate subject having many theories and doctrines but as a common man you need respond to the situation you are placed in and act as per the demand of the situation with all your heart & soul without having any attachment & passion and that is your duty."

"What is my duty now?"

"Keeping above in view ask your own conscience that will guide you properly."

"But I often get confused, mind says something and heart says something else, which one to rely on."

"Whenever, you are in dilemma or you have to chose between different options, always rely on your heart. That would be your inner voice and the true voice which will never confuse you and never betray you."

"Thank you Swamy ji for giving me the light. I will always remember and follow your advice."

Though he had got a clear message, a clear understanding what he was searching for but still he was shooting arrows in the total darkness about what that wealth was ?

He had spent a period of about a month and the money that he had carried with him was near exhaustion and the supervisor of the Dharmashala had also asked him to vacate the place as the same was meant for pilgrims who were visiting the city for holy bath in the Ganges, going around temples & performing Pujas (holy rituals)by staying there for a short duration of time and then going away. He had landed in a new problem of finding a place to stay and to earn his livelihood.

"What should I do to overcome the situation infront of me." he asked his mind.

"Better return back to your parents in your native place and lead a normal life." Replied his mind.

He was not satisfied with the reply he received from his mind. He repeated the same question to his heart.

"No, you stay here and search for the wealth that you are looking for. You find out a job and a place for your stay and continue the search of

that wealth of happiness for which you have set out yourself."

He accepted the advice of the heart and started searching for a job. The city was not still very familiar to him and also he was not known to any one in the city and that was the biggest problem. He had passed higher secondary exam from Maharastra board and was well versed with Marathi language and had working knowledge of English as well but he found that knowledge to be irrelevant in that city for getting any reasonably white collar job despite his best efforts. His heart again advised him to accept any reasonable job and pursue his mission.

One day while wandering near Harishchandra Ghat on the river Ganges and the branch road leading to that he noticed a small milk shop in a corner where an aged person was seen manning the shop however, he noticed hardly a few customers going to that shop. Though having a doubt in his mind of any prospect of employment he went to that shop and asked the person sitting there if he could help him for an employment. The shop owner looked at him from top to toe and with a sense of awe replied if he could work in that shop, however, a meager amount of payment would be made and if he could improve the sales definitely his wages would be increased. Rajesh further enquired about some accommodation to which shop owner showed him a corner place in the shop where he could stay and he could use a nearby public toilet. He accepted the proposal and wished to start the job from next day onwards itself.

Next day after breakfast he came with his bag to the milk shop and joined the job. He kept his bag in the corner as shown to him last day and asked the shop owner about duties that he would have to do. The owner told him all the details about how milk was received from milk vendors in the morning & was processed into different products and how sales were being managed. The shop was being opened early morning and remained open till late in the night, however, on Sundays & festival days shop was being closed in the evenings. He easily understood all the instructions given to him and started working accordingly.

As the days passed by he noticed that there was huge scope and demand of milk and milk products but the shop owner had not used any motivation to customers and also cleanliness was not proper due to which people were not attracted to that shop. He also observed that a number of persons were coming to the ghat to perform funeral rights of their deceased relatives & friends and while returning back after completing cremation they would take some sweets and milk etc and the shop being close to ghat had a big business potential. He started a very tough life. He would get up quite early in the morning and go to public toilet and thereafter take bath in the river Ganges and be ready by six hours in the morning to receive the milk from its suppliers.

He was observing the behavior of milk men very carefully and noticed that they were neither maintaining correct measurement of the milk quantity nor its density due to which the quantity of sales was varying every day and whenever shop owner had enquired about such a thing they always attributed that to the evaporation loss during heating & boiling of the milk in the shop. He told his observations to the master and took his permission to do, whatever, he could to improve upon the things.

He planned to clean thoroughly all the utensils involved & used in the milk business and reorganized the whole thing. In a week's time he completed cleaning of the shop and all equipments & appliances whether big or small and changed the total set-up of the shop to give it a very attractive & decent look.

He purchased measuring bottles and lactometer and testing equipments and started checking the quantity & quality of the milk supplied by different milk men and also testing whether milk was real or chemically prepared one & the density of the milk and recording every thing in a register every day. He performed his testings in the presence of milkmen, record all the observations in their presence and take their signature in the register. There was a lot of hue & cry and resistance by milkmen in the beginning but those honest milkmen appreciated and were happy and willy nilly others also came to terms. Within a fortnight things started showing results and the number of customers swelled up in the shop. The owner appreciated his efforts and was happy.

As the next step he located some widow ladies who were proficient in making different types of sweets. He contacted them for making and supplying certain variety of sweets which were commonly demanded and started selling them with marginal profit. This increased the popularity of the shop and obviously sales and profits as well. Shop owner also responded by increasing his remuneration and reliance on him.

He also started helping the people who were coming to that ghat of Ganges for cremation of dead bodies and performing other funeral ceremonies and all his efforts further increased the popularity of the shop many- folds.

Two months were over and the milk shop had grown in its stature, reputation and business. Two more helping hands had been hired to cater for the increased load. Though he was very happy having got a meaningful life but he was forgetting what for he had come to that city.

One day a grown up girl came to the shop for purchasing some milk and sweets. She appeared to be in the age group of eighteen to twenty years and was good looking. She was wearing clean but ordinary clothes yet there was a mesmerizing radiance on her forehead and face indicating her to be from some good family, however, her eyes were reflecting something of gloom. Rajesh looked at her and felt something but he could not understand what that feeling was? He gave what all she needed and took from her the amount of money as per rates. She left the shop with the articles and went away, however, he continued with his thoughts about her.

Attending to female purchasers and girls was a normal job for him. He had never felt anything about any one of such customers and had been dealing with them in the usual manner with utmost courtesy. It was rather his behavior which had attracted many a new female customers to that shop. But that day, what created a stir in his heart and mind was something new and not at all imagined and also he was not able to understand why, such a thing had happened.

Though over a couple of months had passed by but he was so much so engrossed in the city of Varanasi and the job he was engaged in that he did not find time to know about his mother and father and how had they been at his parental place.

One Sunday evening while sitting at the banks of river Ganges and looking to its serene beauty he thought that the river was considered as PAAP-HARINI(absolving the sins) irrespective of whether some body was a great sinner or an ordinary person. Whosoever, worshipped her with clean feelings & mind and took bath in her pious waters would get absolved of all the sins accumulated by him till then. But why so? Because She was Ganga Maa(mother Ganges), always ready to help her children.

He suddenly remembered that in his childhood school he had been taught that mother was the first god as she not only conceived the child, but from giving birth onwards she took care of every big & small need of the child and ultimately whatever, a child became in his life was due to the blessings, nurturing and prayers of the mother.

He became morose to remember that he also had a mother at his village home who would be weeping for him, would be crying for him, would be worrying for him and would be searching him everywhere and every now & then asking his father about him. While leaving the house he had simply told his parents that he was going to some temple and would be returning back in a couple of days as he had a practice of doing so, they did not mind it but see three months were over of his having left the home and yet he had not given details of his whereabouts and well being to them. What an audacity on his part of having forgotten his own mother and father. He repented and repented and thought that he was also a sinner but will mother Ganges pardon him. Then he thought of first contacting his father, beg for pardon from him and his mother and then solicit pardon from GANGA

MAA.

He immediately got up and went to the nearest public call booth and rang the number of his father's mobile which continued ringing without a response. He tried again after an hour and this time his father responding the call narrated the miserable plight of his mother ever since he had left the home and had not informed of his whereabouts. Rajesh got disturbed to hear all that and begged for pardon. He stated that he was in the city of temples & Ganges - Varanasi and was in search of something and once he got that he would come back. He also assured to send some money to get proper medical treatment of his mother but father asked him to comeback home without worrying for something else.

Next morning when he went to take bath in the Ganges waters he had a totally different feeling praying mother goddess to take care of his mother and pardon him for what all sins he had committed.

The rainy season had commenced and there were sporadic rain falls creating slippery roads and dirty conditions in the city particularly the cow dung getting mixed with water and spreading on the roads giving a very ugly look and also the waters of the river getting mud colored but he noticed people having least worry of all such conditions and leading their life activities unfettered.

He made some very peculiar observations about the city. He noticed there were many centers where old & widow ladies were residing. Though frail and weak yet they were moving freely using bamboo batons and also roads were being used as very peaceful abode

& play ground of co-existence of cows, bulls, dogs and human beings.

People known as Sanyasis wearing saffron robes, carrying pitcher shaped vessels called Kamandals in their hands were also in plenty. In fact he came to know of a proverb regarding that city that only such people could enjoy the city who escaped widows, bulls and Sanyasis. What an amazing thing for any outsider but nothing abnormal for the people of that city.

One Sunday evening, he liked to have a long stroll on the main road and while moving alone on the road he saw white skinned half clad foreigners in plenty also moving on the road who appeared either to be living in the city or being in search of something like him.

****

CHAPTER II

The Love

"Don't indulge in any affair; mind your own business and concentrate on the objective which you are searching for and have come to this place far off from your home town." Said his mind to him.

He seemingly felt satisfied with the advice that came from his mind and he thought of concentrating himself in search of his objective - the wealth, the unknown wealth which could give him happiness. But immediately the advice given to him by Swamy ji in the temple prevailed upon him and he liked to ask his heart, what it had to say?

"Don't ignore your feelings of love, better express it but keep this love chaste and pure away from lust & motives. If you maintain sincerity and purity and don't hesitate to undergo sufferings for that cause you will get a pleasurable life." Advised his heart to him.

He had a great conflict between his mind and heart swinging between two extremes of advices but remembered that heart would always give the true advice, therefore, he decided to accept the same but the biggest dilemma arose how to express that feeling?

He liked to think why such a situation had cropped up that he was put between the conflicts of mind and heart. While having such a thought he went back into the memory lane. Ever since he had come to that milk shop rains had started and the city, its lanes & by lanes, its surroundings and the river waters all had become dirty yet there was no change in the life and the speed of the city movement. Such rains were not uncommon in his native place also, he did not feel anything new but as the days passed by he noticed that on some days there would be very heavy downpour and all the roads would get water logged, everywhere there would be water & water and the river would get swelled up.

He had seen swelling up of river Godawari in his place which would also create havoc and all the area nearby the river would get flooded and submerged but here in Varanasi he saw people enjoying the flooding of river Ganges and the bathing ghats getting shifted to the road sides but the most spectacular sight would be that filth & dirt, garbage and other refuge would be floating and flowing freely and yet people remained undisturbed. They would just splash some water, dispel them away and have their dip. That was a very repulsive sight but the people of that city were so much so used to those that they never felt something abnormal and enjoyed that also as he had earlier also noticed that on the river banks practically every imaginable type of garbage would be floating and just by shifting them away people used to take bath and use Ganges waters.

The same girl who had earlier once purchased milk & other items came to his shop for taking similar items walking on the water-logged road with the same old demeanor, and after taking the items hurriedly went away.

After a couple of days he found that during night when he was fast asleep there had been heavy rains in the hills as well as in the plains consequently all major river would be coming in spate in the plains. And lo!after a few days river Ganges started rising and that time the water level was going up very fast and people near the banks and other low lying areas were getting panicky and were being shifted to safer places. The water current was very fast and the river was looking like an ocean, an endless ocean of water current. Anything coming in the way of the water current was getting swept away and it was not possible to stop that. Water level had come up to his shop floor level and still it was likely to go up. He had placed an old wooden table for sleeping in the night but his neighbors had advised him to be vigilant & careful and in case of any emergency he could shift to the upper floor where many other working men were residing.

Next day morning when he woke up he found that fortunately water had remained constant but warning from district authorities was continuing of situation getting still worse and all his neighbors and others had become careful to face any eventuality but their daily routine had got badly disturbed as the public toilet had got inundated, municipal water supply had got badly affected, electricity supply was practically absent and a large number of people had made the lower ebb of water on the road as the bathing ghat.

The milk vendors were also not coming regularly and its receipt was much lower than normally it used to be and the processing of milk and its products had also become difficult & irregular though demand still existed as usual.

That day he could organize his shop very late in the morning and had very limited quantity of milk available for sale. Mid-day noon was approaching but that day only a few customers had come till then to purchase milk that suddenly he noticed the same girl coming to his shop. She came to the shop, purchased a limited quantity of milk and started going back. She had lifted her sari above the ankle and was wearing a pair of ordinary rubber chappals. She had hardly moved a few steps that her chappal slipped on the road and she fell in the water. Before she could balance herself and stand up, a small ripple of water came and she got dragged towards the river side. Some people standing nearby noticed her and shouted for help but none of them rushed to help her.

Hearing the loud noise he came out of the shop and saw the plight of the girl. Without wasting any time and giving a second thought he jumped into the water and rushed towards her but she was getting dragged towards the river side, which had made her upset and totally disturbed. Within a minute he could reach her and held her tightly in his arms but he was getting displaced due to heavy flow of water. Fortunately a person who was seeing all that got a rope from somewhere and holding its end in his hands threw the other end towards Rajesh.

This acted like a straw to a drowning person and both of them tried to catch that rope. In the meantime some others also joined at the other end and pulled the rope held by Rajesh and the girl to safety.

Thank God! something which could have become disastrous was averted by the prudence of luck. Though rescued, the girl was badly frightened, terrified and was in shambles. Neither she was able to speak to thank her rescuers nor the God! nor was she able to move ahead. She remained sitting at a wooden plank given to her by someone while he and some others tried to comfort her.

After a lapse of about fifteen minutes time she regained herself and liked to go back home but in the melee she had lost her milk packet. He rushed to the shop & took out another milk packet, locked the shop, came to her and gave the milk packet and offered to escort her up to her residence.

On reaching her house she thanked him profusely for all the help and saving her life, however, while expressing her gratitude she used some words which were of Marathi language and they were totally unfamiliar to the local people who knew Bhojpuri and Hindi. He got a shock as to how come! she used Marathi language but without any further talks she went inside the house and he moved back to his shop.

He reopened the shop and started back the routine, however, under the continuing threat of swelling river and of course a new thought about the girl whether she was really a Maharastrian and if so, how was she here in Varanasi and why was she having a sorrowful demeanor? But the threat of flooded river was so much so that he concentrated more on saving himself and his shop than anything else. And see! the fear came true, by the evening the flood waters entered the shop and he consequently with his essential belongings decided to move to the first floor to stay with other workmen already staying there.

Next morning when he got up he found rains in the city and attending to daily routine being very difficult, however, like others he also managed the show. Along with some men he went to the roof top of the house to see, how the flood situation was looking like.

Oh! it was fearsome, dreaded, horrible, thundering and roaring of the vast water current. The river was flowing very fast having inundated a vast portion of city and villages & other localities on the other side of it. He saw a large number of uprooted trees, thatched roofs, animal carcasses and dead human bodies and many other things getting afloat in the water current. It was really a pathetic sight. He immediately thought if river Ganges was emancipator of sins then why such a cruel act that it was sweeping across destroying vegetation, crops, trees, homes & hearth of those who came in the way of the flooded waters and cattle & human beings. What wrong had they all done to meet with such a fate that there was no formal cremation to those dead human bodies floating & flowing in the river? Oh! sad, so sad.

He got choked with emotions and feelings for all those who might have been helpless & hapless to meet their bitter and tragic end and heart to heart he started cursing the river for having forgotten her benefactor role.

While thinking so, the episode of the

last day flashed to his mind and he trembled to imagine that had timely help not been available to that girl, the Marathi knowing girl, she would have probably also met a similar fate as he saw many dead bodies floating in the river waters.

His chain of thoughts was broken by the sounds of foot steps of other companions who were getting down to start their daily chores of work to the extent that was possible. He also followed the suit and came down, but there was no milk supplier having come till then and shop being filled with water there was no scope for organizing the shop activities.

The situation remained as such for two days after which water started receding leaving mud & filth behind but still some water was there on the road. The cleaning of the shop and its surrounding was a difficult job coupled with cleaning of all the utensils & appliances which took one full day only after which the shop activities could be brought back to normalcy.

After a week the water had gone to the river bed though it was full to the brim at the banks, that municipal authorities announced everyone to observe extreme care as there was fear of epidemic and advised absolute cleanliness and use of bottled or boiled water for drinking & cooking purposes and also advised people to refrain from entering the river waters at least for a couple of days unless & until it was absolutely essential like doing cremation etc.

In a week's time normalcy had returned back and the life had become as usual but for him the flood had left many scars behind which would frighten him and disturb him sometimes even in dreams.

One day again he rang his father and narrated to him the horrible experiences what all he had during the past few days who again asked him to come back home. His mother also spoke on the phone and weepingly asked him to leave things as such and be back home, however, he assured them in his usual manner to be back soon.

A fortnight had elapsed and the people of city had practically forgotten the floods & the havoc it had caused and the damage it had done to the city, people of the city and who all came in the flood waters in the range of the river.

The same girl again came to the shop for purchasing some milk & sweets. No sooner he saw her, something happened to him but he could not understand what that was; but one thing which he strongly felt was to ask her how she knew Marathi language but before he could speak she herself spoke,

"I am grateful for your courage and help to save me on that day. I will never forget that."

"I tried to do what a person should have done to help someone in distress, however, please tell me how do you know Marathi language as no one knows that here."

"I know just a few words and nothing more."

"That I can't believe. There is a typical accent which you showed while I had escorted you to your home that day."

"Oh! So you know that."

"Yes, because I am myself a Maharastrian. Your accent indicated yourself to be from somewhere near Bhusawal or that area."

"You are possibly right but it is my destiny that I am here. Though I have learnt the local

language and Hindi very well but accent is something which won't change."

"Will you tell me, how are you here and how long?"

"Some other day. Actually I don't like to open the chapter which is closed long back and in fact it is very painful for me to go back to those days."

"Alright, as you like."

She took the requisite items and went away having kindled a spark in his mind that she was from a place located somewhere near to his home place but question remained, what made her become a native of Varanasi since she was not wearing any vermilion on her forehead indicating her to be spinster.

She came to the shop next day but without talking anything she collected the requisite items and went away. This became a normal practice that she would come everyday to the shop and take the items. One day the other helpers were not present in the shop and Rajesh was all alone that she enquired about where from he belonged to,

"I am from Nasik, a village about twenty kilometers away from the city on the banks of river Godavari."

"Oh! wonderful my mother also belonged to Nasik but I don't remember what exactly that place is."

"How long are you here in this city?"

"For about fifteen, sixteen years."

"Who all are here with you?"

"My mother, in fact the mother who has adopted me."

"Why, why? where is your real mother."

"She has become a star in the sky."

"What do you mean?"

"She is no more."

"But what about your real father?"

"He is also no more."

"Any brother or sister."

"No one."

She did not talk any further and left the shop. His strange feelings towards her were getting stronger and stronger but he was not able to know what to do and willy-nilly continued with that unchanged and she also continued as usual coming to the shop and purchasing the items. One day she looked a little different and after taking items from the shop asked him,

"My mother likes to meet you, can you come to our house?"

"Why not, I shall come there on coming Sunday evening."

As promised he visited their house the very next Sunday.

"Come in my son, Rajani has told me about you." Greeted him an elderly voice as he knocked at the door.

"Thank you Mata ji(mother)." He took out his shoes at the door outside and entered the house barefoot.

The house located in a lane was small and quite ordinary but it was very clean, neat & tidy and was brimming with purity and piousness. There was a small room full of deities, photographs of gods & goddesses and many types of books where a small earthen-ware lamp was lit and incense stick was burning emitting a pleasant fragrance.

"I have called you to personally thank you for saving the life of Rajani. In fact you did a dare devil act to save her from the clutches of a disastrous situation." She asked him to sit

in an old chair lying in the inside verandah of the house. He occupied the chair and thankfully replied,

"I did what any gentleman should have done and nothing more."

"I understand you are familiar with Nasik in Maharastra."

"Yes. I belong to that area."

"I have also been to that area several times along with Sashtri ji. We were frequent visitors of Trayambkeshwar for conducting different types of puja(rituals of worship)and visiting Lord Shiva temple."

"I have also been to that temple several times."

"Oh good, very good. Nasik is a very good place, what brings you here to this city."

"My destiny."

They had a fairly long discussion about various things of Trayambkeshwar, the birth place of Lord Hanuman which is a few kilometers away from there and different types of rituals which are performed only in that place and also the life of people of that area which brought them closer to know and understand each other.

The management of shop by Rajesh had brought it to a big business and it had added sale of several other products. The shop owner was supervising in the mornings & evenings and taking account in the morning for the proceeds of last day. He was pleased to find him very honest and having maintained everything transparent & clear.

Rajani was regularly coming to the shop and exchanging pleasantries. One Sunday evening when he had gone to her house to meet Mata ji, after having discussions he was asked to take Rajani some day to Lord Vishwanath temple and to the banks of river Ganges as she was mostly confined to the limited and closed space of the house and accordingly it was fixed for the coming Sunday afternoon.

The beauty of Varanasi lay in the narrow serpentine lanes, crowds, beggars, old widow ladies clad in whitish clothes, cows & other animals roaming freely and of course pleasing sights along the ghats of river Ganges.

Rajesh and Rajani went to the Vishwanath temple first to pray Lord Shiva and thereafter traversing through the thick crowds of the roads they came to a serene place on the banks of the river which was cool, calm and tranquil. They sat side by side and fortunately that place was not much frequented then by people coming to & fro to Ganges.

He had been continuously haunted by the thought that she knew Marathi language and was an adopted child of Shastri couple but how did that happen? And therefore, he liked to get that chapter opened but without hurting her sentiments .

"The other day you said that your mother has become a star in the sky, what about your father, is he also a star in the sky?"

"Yes. He has also become a star in the sky."

"Do you recognize them?"

"No, I don't recognize them. There are thousands & thousands of stars in the sky, somewhere in their midst they are also placed in the sky."

"Do you communicate with them."

"Yes. Though I can not identify & recognize them but definitely they recognize me.

Whenever, I feel sad I look to the sky in the night when sky is clear of clouds, I call them, I weep to them, I explain to them my problems and I solicit their blessings and they respond immediately. Something happens and my sorrow is taken care of."

"But how did you get such an idea?"

"My foster father Shastri ji was a very learned man, he was a great astrologer. Whenever, I asked him about my parents he told me that they are there in the sky as stars and always they look to me."

"Does every one become a star after death?"

"No. Only those who have been good & virtuous people they after their death become stars in the sky but those who have not been good they suffer even after leaving the world."

"You see, this majestic river Ganges flowing endlessly & called as emancipator of sinners, what about fishes & other aquatic creatures in this river?"

"Such people who were sinners in their previous birth but realized it and repented for that they become fishes etc and find an abode in this sacred river so that they could get emancipated."

"But what about those who were sunk deep into sins and unholy deeds and also never repented for them?"

"There are many different types of YONIMS (birth creations) where they go after their death, some become ghosts & evil spirits, some become different types of animals and of course some become unholy human beings also depending on the quantum & type of sins committed by them and they continue doing that even in their present birth also and suffer for their misdeeds endlessly through series of births & deaths."

"Good, let us be careful not to commit sins. But see after death the dead body is consigned to flames or to electric furnace and burnt off, then how somebody goes to different YONIMS."

"Our Hindu mythology believes that SOUL which is the part of supreme cosmic energy and is responsible for our being in the present form is IMMORTAL & INDESTRUCTIBLE. Only physical body dies and same is cremated. Once soul is relieved of this body it goes to some other Yonim and takes another embodiment, however, depending on the Karmas (deeds) accumulated from previous births plus Karmas performed through the embodiment which they left."

"Then how your parents could become stars and have not taken another birth?"

"As I have already told you they were good and virtuous people."

On that day Rajesh could understand why so many stars were there in the sky. But simultaneously he felt happy that so many good people had been born & they lived on the earth who were stars then. However he liked to continue his discussions further,

"*You said that Shastri ji was a great astrologer, how do you know that ?*"

"*Though he was a priest in the famous KAL BHAIRAV (a fierce form of Lord Shiva) temple in the city but he was conducting classes also for teaching astrology and had many disciples. Many people were coming to him for knowing many things about their fate & future and every body used to say that whatever he advised or predicted was cent per cent correct.*"

"*Did he tell something about you?*"

"*Nothing much.*"

"*Did he teach you astrology?*"

"*Yes, for the last two years of his life. Earlier he kept me away from this and always asked me to concentrate on my studies. I did that and have passed my graduation in social sciences but two years before his death suddenly he asked me to be with him and study astrology.*"

"Have you become proficient in astrology?"

"Not to the level he wanted. He taught me starting from all the basics to deep details in those two years. In fact, everything big or small is contained in the stars and astrology is pure science like astronomy but there are certain things which are hidden and they don't easily appear on the horoscope of a person. Shastri ji told me that intuition and power to see piercing through the expanse of time was vital to know those hidden details. He taught me the science of stars and was beginning to give me the insight to see through the times that suddenly he died and that part I could not learn."

"Did you not try to learn those things from some one else available in the city."

"No. He was the only person who knew those things and once he had told me that such details were given only to worthy son or daughter or disciple and not to any body else."

"Did he not train some one of his disciples."

"No. He did not find somebody good for that, however, while examining my forehead he one day found me suitable for astrology and giving the advanced knowledge."

"Did he tell you something before his death.?"

"Yes. He told me that I have to bear some unexpected responsibility but that would not be for a long period. He also told me that one day I will reach somewhere in the vicinity of my home place, but he did not indicate me something about that and also when and how?"

"That is really wonderful."

"One thing more, he also told me that God! never does something without a purpose and whatever happens is as per His planning & there is nothing like coincidence or accident but He never tells anything beforehand, however, those who can read the good and bad omens can guess something of the coming events."

"It means my meeting with you is also a

part of cosmic planning and has some purpose."

"Definitely."

The discussions were quite illuminating. He could understand that his coming to Varanasi was not a coincidence but some planning of the God and meeting with Rajani had also some purpose, but what that could be? However, he immediately remembered that God never told something beforehand and things came when time was due for them. Nevertheless, still he was curious to know the circumstances why she was there in Varanasi and he gathered some courage and asked her,

"You have given me some divine knowledge but please don't mind, my curiosity is to know what has made you come to this city and be with Shastri ji and his wife."

"There is a tragic story buried in the grave of past but probably that is my fate to repeat it to

you. My father was an affluent person having a lot of properties near Jalgaon district in Maharastra state. Our family consisted of my mother & father, my elder brother and myself. My brother was ten years elder to me. I was five years old then. Our parents and we were on way to Vaishno Devi shrine near Jammu traveling by train in an air conditioned coach. Shastri couple joined us at New Delhi station. They occupied two berths near our berths. Shastri ji had started some inquiries about us which made us quite informal. We had a very pleasant journey, chit chatting and sharing eatables together. We reached Jammu and therefrom also we went to the shrine together and fortunately on our return journey also we got berths together near to each other. This had created quite a good understanding amongst us. On way back our train steamed off from Jammu Tavi railway station at nine hours in the night. We took our dinner and slept after an hour. Around midnight I had got up to go to bathroom but then I was surprised to find Shastris not being

on their berths, possibly they had alighted on
some station mid-way when we were fast asleep.
Thereafter I was in half sleep that around three
hours in the morning there was a big bang and
after that what all happened I don't know
except that when I came to senses I found four
bogies ahead of our bogie completely mutilated
& damaged and a large number of people
wounded & crying. Though none appeared
surviving in those four bogies but only ten dead
bodies were shown to media the next day. I
found my mother & father also dead but my
brother was not found either among survivors or
among wounded. I was crying & crying and like
me there were many more but none was there to
help us and whatever help came that was too late
to save some people who could have been saved. I
was given first aid & shifted to a remand home.
After some days some of our relatives came who
claimed the dead bodies of my mother and father
and took them away for cremation but they all
refused to recognize me despite my repeated
requests.

Subsequently they claimed the compensation also. I could neither get to know of my brother nor of my fate. After a month Shastri couple came to the remand home and legally adopted me and brought me to their home. They always treated me like their own daughter and did every thing what parents do. Unfortunately a year back Shastri ji while conducting some rituals in the temple had a massive pain in the chest and while on way to hospital he died. He was a very pious & chaste person not having accumulated any wealth and consequently mother's responsibility has fallen on me. With the knowledge of astrology whatever I am having I am able to earn something and some of disciples also help us and that is how we are managing our livelihood. Our neighbor had great respect for Shastri ji and they also take care of us."

"Oh my God, you are having a painful story. I suppose you must have seen your fate & fortune and what all awaits you in future."

"No; one should not study about himself as

that is not desirable in astrology but intuition will caution if something adverse is coming ahead. Probably Shastri ji could see something after having boarded the train when we were returning from Jammu and alighted from the train at some earlier station and also might be he had seen something about me. But to my misfortune he could not give me that knowledge."

"Did Shastri ji leave behind something for the future of your mother and yourself."

"He did not leave behind any money, however, we found after his death that he had made a will that after his death the house where we live and is ancestral house will go to Mrs.Shastri and if something happened to her then it will come to me but if I marry it would go the KAL BHAIRAV temple trust and would be converted into an institute of astrology. He has named some of his disciples who will take care of the proposed institute."

The dusk time was nearing and crowd of visitors was gradually swelling up on the river banks and they decided to return back home.

He had a good time with Rajani and that company had reinforced in him that he had a very soft corner for her, may be that was love for her. While heart was advising him to express his feelings to her without wasting any time, he had not been able to muster enough courage to express the same and was still swinging in the conflict between mind and heart.

CHAPTER III

The Truth Hidden

"Things may not always be the same and therefore I should express my love to Rajani but how to do that? I don't know of her mind and if things go wrong then I will get hurt."

He was in a great conflict with himself. Every time he met her his heart advised him to express his feelings towards her but somehow he could not, however, from his behavior she had already guessed his feelings and was ready to respond him affirmatively provided he took the lead but that was not coming forth.

The fury of rainy season was over and the fortnight of Mahalaya popularly known as Shraddh Paksh had commenced. The city had a very austere environ as every Hindu was busy in remembering his ancestors and doing various rituals for them.

Every morning he would see people

coming to different ghats of Ganges, taking holy dip in the river and performing the rituals on the banks of the river and thereafter feeding beggars, birds and cows. Though things were full of sanctity but those were increasing the rubbish all around haphazardly.

That was a very bad period for Rajani as there was no male member available in the family line for performing the rights in respect of her own real parents and also for late Shastri ji as that period was sacrosanct for every Hindu to worship the forefathers meticulously following the procedures as specified by the scriptures lest the non-performance of specified rituals etc., was apprehended to invite wrath of the ancestors. That abnormal situation had forced her to do herself the specified rituals as long as she could be permitted by religious tenets.

He had become very careful and every morning himself would deliver the milk packets at her residence.

The sale of milk and sweets had gone abnormally high, however, with the help of two assistants he was managing the show and the owner of the shop was also giving more time for business activities. The last day of the Mahalaya was specially important as on that day the souls of all the ancestors would be offered their choicest food items, they would be ceremoniously worshiped and once every ritual was over, they were supposed to go back to their heavenly abode to return back to earth only next Mahalaya period.

On that day all the ghats of Ganges were flooded with family members and priests, all busy in performing rituals & ceremonies and of course beggars were there also in plenty. Mrs.Shastri and

Rajani accompanied with the disciples of late Shastri ji had also come to a ghat and performed all the ceremonies. They all were in tears as they had lost the most valuable pillar of their life but everyone was sincerely praying for the soul of late Shastri ji to bestow blessings for all good things on them.

Next day onwards the nine auspicious days of NAVARATRI commenced which was the most sacred period meant for worship of mother goddess DURGA and Lord Rama - the period of celebration of victory of good over the evil.

There came a total paradox of all that he had observed during the bygone fortnight and the whole city and people in it wore the festive look. Ramlila and Durgapuja were organized at numerous places and the entire city had become a big congregation of festivities, celebrations and religious activities. Those things were a little different for him as he had not witnessed such a large scale activities in his native place. Though everywhere the mood of happiness & gaiety pervaded but he noticed that a pal of gloom was looming large over Rajani and her mother. One day when she had come to collect milk, that he suddenly asked her,

"Why do you look so sad and morose when the whole of city is happy, is it due to the demise of your parents?"

"No, parents had to go one day on their journey to eternity and they have gone; that was natural, only that they met with an undesirable tragic demise. Though that gives me pains but really I feel sad for my brother, had I known that he was dead I would have tried to forget him and would have conducted ceremonies for him last fortnight as I did for others but I don't know where is he, whether he is dead or alive?"

"But one day you had told me that Shastri ji had made all possible efforts to trace out & locate him but all in vain then why don't you take it for granted that he is no more."

"I understand & that may be the fact also but my heart is still not ready to accept that. Unfortunately I could not see his dead body and government sources also did not come out with any fact about him though we had confirmed reservations and therefore still I feel he may be somewhere."

"Pray God! almighty and leave rest to Him. If you are destined, he may meet you, wherever, he may be."

That day he realized the strength of heart and he decided to express his feelings to her no sooner he got the opportunity when she was not gloomy and no body else was there in the shop.

The season of festivities and celebrations continued for a period of one month under one or the other pretext that gradually cold weather started knocking at the doors and the temperature began dipping down & down as the days passed by.

The month of January witnessed a very rough weather when for a number of days city was engulfed practically under freezing temperature with mist converting daytime into darkness. The river water had become too cold to bathe and the mist had made entire sky and river bed looking like an endless ocean having its expanse from earth to sky.

He was feeling extreme pinch of cold which was an entirely new experience for him and also that he was not having enough warm clothing to face such a weather.

One day he rang his father and narrated the condition and the plight which he was undergoing in that city and again his father and mother both repeated the same demand for him to come back home.

Though he had a mind to see his mother who was not keeping a good health but he had then an additional pull of Rajani and was not going to miss her without having expressed his love to her, however, either the time was not benign or he was failing to muster enough courage to speak out whenever such near opportunities came to him.

Winter had been very cruel to him and when the cold wind started coming from the frozen north he felt even his bones having got frozen particularly during the night hours. He purchased some cheap warm clothing from the road side vendors who had come from the mountain regions of the north and were popularly referred to as PAHARIS and also he noticed that at many vantage points dried wood logs were being burnt for generating heat and the people like him were getting warmth from the heat of burning wood and strength to fight cold pervading the area.

However, he noticed that Rajani was coming wearing some warm clothing but not much disturbed with the extreme cold of the place. One day he simply asked her,

"Now whole city is shivering and the people are trembling with the cold, how are you maintaining yourself so normal?"

"There is a simple secret. We take warm milk, with some nutmeg powder dissolved in it before we go to bed to sleep in the night and this gives us enough heat in the body which enables us to face the cold weather. In fact during fifteen & odd years I have seen still bitter cold and am now used to it but definitely for any person like you this is a horrible situation."

"Do you think, there is some inner strength which helps anyone to face whatever odds he is placed in."

She laughed & laughed very heartily showing her pearl white teeth and a very decorous demeanor with her thin lips just opened up & stretched wide, something which was very unusual for her and she spontaneously said,

"The word inner strength is a mysterious word and is used by those who are either not in a position to afford something or do something & yet shown to stand strong or by those who are having firm determination to achieve their cherished objectives ahead of them or by those who have gone much above the normal human beings and have become detached & dispassionate."

"But you know great Shivaji had a powerful inner strength which enabled him to conquer so many battles with a handful of army and establish a vast Hindu empire."

"He was not a normal human being but a man of firm determination and also his mother & Guru were behind him in making him what he came to be."

"Do you feel I have some inner strength that I am able to withstand this inclement weather condition?"

"That is physical endurance arisen out of circumstances you are placed in and that is not the inner strength."

"Oi re deva (Oh, my God)!" She abruptly terminated the discussions and went away saying that she was in a hurry.

However, he had landed in a catch twenty two situation whether he had inner strength or not. Though he apparently maintained himself cool & busy in his usual business but his mind was continuously debating on that point and at length he realized that he lacked inner strength otherwise there was an opportunity for him to express his feelings to her which he had missed and it may not be easy to get some other opportunity like that.

That night he could not sleep well and remained deep into thoughts about his own weaknesses. He continued wandering into the wonderland of memories, the memories which were so intense that he totally forgot anything else other than them.

He remembered that he was a small child living with his father & mother who were too affectionate to him. He had a very pleasant life with his parents. He used to go to village school where he was being taught through Marathi medium. His mother was a very good cook and he was always fond of sweet rice prepared by her. His father was having some farmland which was being used for cultivation of grape vines and vegetables.

As the hot months approached the grapes in vineyard would ripen emitting a sweet fragrance and very sweet taste. His father would pluck the grape bunches place them carefully in a basket and take it to the nearest market where he would deliver that to the merchant.

On Sundays & other holidays his father would take him to the nearest place on the main road, spread a mat on the side berm and put a stall of grapes & other vegetables plucked from his farms and mostly small vehicle passengers would stop there and purchase those fresh items giving much higher price than what his father used to get by selling them to the merchant in the market.

River Godawari was hardly a kilometer away from his village and he along with his village friends would go to the river occasionally where children would play and swim in the river waters.

During summers water would not be much and the river would look like a very narrow streak of water, however, during rains same would swell up and a large area on both sides of the banks would get inundated & submerged but he remembered that expanse of river Godavari was not at all comparable to the expanse of Ganges what he saw during floods at Varanasi.

River Godavari was also considered as pious as the Ganges and there would be occasions of holy dip near the city of Nasik where he had seen several bathing ghats made of concrete steps as he saw at Dashaswamedh ghat at Varanasi and also there used to be KUMBH after every twelve years.

As he was going down the memory lane his eyes got filled with tears, he started sobbing and got his throat choked with emotions,

"Oh Baba(father) how much I miss you, my Aai(mother) how and when will I get the sweets made by you. Unnecessarily I have taken a plunge to search for something which neither I know nor can guess and when would I get that but definitely I am feeling the pinch of your absence, my Aai and Baba."

Emotions had so much so overpowered him that he continued sobbing & weeping and when did he ultimately sleep, he could not remember.

Next morning he got up little late and only then he realized that last night had been too difficult for him. However, he swung into action to get ready before the milk vendors came to the shop.

The other two helpers belonged to some village located on the other side of the river and were coming late and were also going away early in the evening and consequently early morning and late night jobs were still his responsibility.

One morning a person came to the shop for purchasing some sweets & milk whom he was seeing for the first time. The person was strange looking and his attire was also not conforming to what he had seen local people wearing, however, he simply asked for the requisite items, paid for them and went away.

Next day onwards he saw him coming to the shop every day and purchasing the same items, however, that person seemed very inquisitive and used to look at the shop with searching eyes, noticing the cleanliness of the shop, its business management and the courtesy with which customers were being attended to. Apparently he seemed impressed but never expressed anything.

Suddenly one day he asked one of the helpers,

"I find that things have been beautifully managed here who is the person doing all this?"

Helper pointed out towards Rajesh who simply nodded his head. He further said that,

"Varanasi is not that big a city and this shop is also very small, I am impressed with the way whole things are being managed here, I can get a better opportunity for you in a similar business in Kolkata. I am here for a few days more and you can consider and let me know your acceptance or otherwise or whenever, you feel like you can ring me." He told Rajesh and went away.

Next three days he continued his purchases as usual, however, on the fourth day he called Rajesh and gave him his visiting card & all other details and told him that he was leaving the city on that day in the evening but he could be contacted and conveyed acceptance of his proposal on his mobile phone. Thereafter that gentleman was not seen in that shop and gradually he was forgotten.

A period of more than eight months had passed of his stay in Varanasi, he had taken a small rented room near the shop and had settled there very well but still Rajesh was not able to locate & find the wealth which he had been searching for and was becoming restive.

Every time he made a ring to his father, he would be asked by his mother to come back home & take care of her as her health was gradually deteriorating and his absence was giving her extreme agony and pains. He was in a fix between the pulls of his mother, Rajani and his own quest. His mind was always advising him to return back home without worrying for other things but his heart was advising him the other way round to express his feelings to her without worrying for the outcome and to make at least one more effort to find out what was he looking for.

This inner war between his mind and the heart continued for about a month. Days passed by without any change in the situation that one day Rajani, when she came to the shop, was seen totally emotionless on her face and just having taken the things was to go back, that he asked her,

"I have never seen you like this, what makes you so? I know that despite all odds of life you have always maintained yourself calm and composed, then why so to-day?"

She did not seem to be in a mood to reply to his question and turned back to go but he called her and insisted to know. She simply said,

"I am feeling very lonely and am not able to see the light of the day. I had a bad dream last night and saw myself being swept away in the strong current of the flooded Ganges and there was no one to help me despite my continuous crying for help. Those who were visible on the banks were behaving just as spectators as if seeing a dead body floating&flowing. I was trying to locate you for help but I did not see you in the crowd. This is a bad omen and while looking to certain horoscopes I felt that something wrong is in offing which may happen to me or to someone known to me."

"Oh, that is the reason. Don't take that by heart; every dream is not a foreteller. Remember, what had happened during the flooding of the Ganges when you had come to this shop & had got slipped in the river waters and probably that is still haunting your mind. But one thing, take it for granted that I will never let you down and never leave you helpless. In fact I love you and really love you from the core of my heart."

She was totally stunned, totally astonished to listen to that and instantaneously spoke,

"Deva re deva (Oh, my God!)" and without even looking back she went away.

****

CHAPTER IV

Towards Realities

*H*e was traveling in a reserved three tier sleeper coach from Varanasi to Howrah in the super fast train having left Cantt station in the evening. That was a reasonably comfortable compartment where he could sit comfortably and would sleep in the night without any problem and there was no unwanted crowd. He had paid much more extra money to get a reservation in that train but he was happy that he would not repeat the experiences what he had while coming to Varanasi from his Nasik Road station.

Around eight hours in the night most of the co-passengers started taking their tiffin or dinner whatever they had brought with them. He also opened his bag, took out the tiffin box, opened it and took the rice & curry what he had brought with him. He finished his food and then took the tiffin box to the water tap located near the entrance of the compartment, cleaned it, wiped with a towel, closed the lid and kept that in the bag and then closed the bag which he was going to use as a pillow while sleeping on the berth.

Once the dinner was over some of the passengers started chit-chatting about the dangers en-route as the train would be passing through the Naxalite infested area during the dead of night and each one advised the other one to keep their belongings carefully and ensure that the doors at the entrance were properly locked.

One person occupying the side way berth narrated a horrible story which had happened a few days back when a group of Naxalites attacked the train in the dead of the night, opened the entrance gate of a compartment and had killed a number of innocent persons after which security had been beefed up but it was better to be careful.

The passengers spread their cloth sheets on their respective berths and spread themselves on them. He also lied down on his berth but he could not go to sleep as more than safety of himself in the journey, he was deeply drowned in the memories of Varanasi which he had bade good bye only a few hours back.

"Is it Rajesh, then come in door is not locked from inside, just push in and open." He heard the sound of Mataji when he had come to meet her one Sunday evening and had knocked at the door.

He entered the house, wished the elderly lady and sat on the mat lying spread near her.

"Mataji, you called me; something special."He asked.

"Yes. Rajani told me that you are planning to leave the city and go else where."

"Yes. That is true."

"But, why?"

"That is my destiny. I came to this city unmindfully but here I learnt that I was in search of something which could get me happiness. I have done my best but I could not get that. I have to continue my search hereafter in the city of joy-Kolkata."

"This is the place where people come from everywhere in the world in search of peace, tranquility and emancipation and freedom from the bondage of birth & death and you after having established yourself, are going to leave the place. I am not able to believe it, if there is something haunting you, why don't you tell me?"

"No, nothing else. In fact, I have got a lot of love from you and I never felt lonely here but I could not make myself satisfied from inside and that makes me continue my search further."

"I still feel, this place may give you whatever, you are searching for."

"But somehow I feel that I must go ahead."

"Ok. Once you have made up your mind, I will not ask you to stop your search, but definitely I will request you to keep us always in your mind and before you go away better you take Rajani to Sarnath one day and show her the Buddha Vihar."

"I will do that this Sunday."

He stayed there for about an hour and had a long discussion with her mother and then left for his place.

He took Rajani on Sunday to Sarnath and after entering the Buddha Vihar they had the first encounter with the majestic Chaukhandi Stupa built by the great emperor Asoka-the-great to commemorate the first sermons of Dhamma delivered by Buddha-the-enlightened to his five disciples. They took a round of various relics of the Viharas, then went to a nearby restaurant to take some tiffin. They came thereafter to the famous deer park and spent sometimes to watch the beautiful deers therein. Both of them decided to sit in the shade of a big tree and watch the deers while enjoying some eatables.

While watching the deers they spotted a pair of deers who were little darker in color, were looking very beautiful and were grazing and playing together. They were so affectionate to each other, licking & hugging each other through their neck and seeing eye to eye passionately that they attracted the attention of Rajesh and Rajani. They remained watching them and while watching their activities they forgot themselves. She remembered the story of two black bucks as mentioned in the Buddhist Jatakas Tales, their love and sacrifices made for the good of others.

"I too love you. The other day you had expressed your love to me, to-day is my turn." Suddenly spoke Rajani to him.

Though he was surprised the way that expression had come so abruptly, however, somewhere in the deepest corner of his heart he had nurtured that ambition and obviously it was something of greatest delight seeing his desire getting fulfilled.

"To-day I am really happy. I have been searching for that secret wealth which could give me happiness and now you have given me that." But immediately he controlled himself,

"but whatever you have given to me is just a part of that wealth and still I have to search for the thing which can give me total happiness."

"Oh my God! so still you are looking for something more?"

"Yes."

"But what about our love?"

"That will continue endlessly, but can you wait for?"

"How long?"

"Not much. See as for as I am concerned I can wait for you through out my life but I will not make you wait for long. I am going away to another city but we will be continuously in touch with each other. If I succeed well and good otherwise I will come back and join you in permanent bondage and try to make others happy."

"Ok .That is good. I will wait but why not fix an year as the limit."

That was the most valuable moment of his life and its memory was good enough to enrich his whole life but he was perplexed that what else was he searching for when he had already got a great wealth in form of Rajani? Then he thought that when he was coming to Varanasi, he was totally in darkness but he learnt so many things and also got something so valuable, may be destiny had something hidden in store for him at the new place he was going to.

His happiness disappeared with the flash of memory while he had decided to leave the milk shop and how everyone was sad when he came out with his proposal to go away. The owner of the shop was in shambles with the idea of his departure away and his two assistants were also in deep pains.

In the manner he had brought up the dilapidated shop to a blossomed business, his honesty, sincerity, courteousness and introduction of new systems and his popularity among customers had given a boost to the management of the shop and all those measures had been beyond the imagination of the shop owner who had repeatedly asked him to reconsider his going away but he had respectfully acknowledged the help which he had received when he was an unknown entity in that city and assured him to maintain relations wherever he was.

Sinking and floating in the ocean of memories when did he get asleep he could not know and only about two hours in the morning he got up to go to toilet to ease himself.

He found that all the passengers were fast asleep and the train was running at a very high speed producing a lot of rattling and noise. He came back to his top berth and spread himself to sleep again. He was going ahead in half sleep dreaming of so many things good and bad that suddenly there was a big explosion like sound and he felt as if the train had jumped high and he had fallen down with a thud & everything was in darkness. He could not understand what had happened that there started coming sounds of screaming, crying and people weeping in deep pains. He felt a lot of burden on his head and people around him shouting for help.

After a few minutes he realized that something undesirable had happened and the train had met with some serious accident and his bogie had fallen somewhere down below the railway track. He found himself very close to the entrance gate which was totally shattered. He tried to lift up his body but there was deep pain in his legs, however, somehow he lifted himself up and dragged himself out of the damaged bogie.

He saw some people from nearby area rushing with lantern and torches etc who came to the spot and whatever help they could, they started rendering to the passengers in distress. How much time passed by he could not assess that he saw some people having come with trucks & lorries. They hurriedly started taking out human bodies from the front bogies and loading them in the trucks. Those trucks were taken away and such operations continued till there was light in the eastern horizon heralding the onset of the dawn. As the sun rose in the eastern sky he saw that the entire train had met with very serious accident and the front few bogies were totally gone off.

Around nine hours in the morning a relief train arrived with medical and other facilities, media men and railway officials also arrived at the scene of accident. He found himself quite fit only having some injuries in his limbs for which some medical aid was given on the spot and he was to wait for alternate arrangement along with many other such passengers.

The accident site presented a very-very ghastly scene, still many mutilated bodies were lying near the damaged train bogies. He met with some villagers who were first to run to the help and they told him that,

"some Naxalites would have blown the railway track only some minutes before this train was to pass through that area due to which the train while in full speed might have gone off. The front five, six bogies had got totally damaged beyond any hope of survivors, however, by the time media men came hardly fifty dead bodies were available on the accident site. In the night policemen had come from the nearest post and they had loaded all dead bodies whatever they could find in the darkness of night, in the trucks and by now they all would have been thrown in the river Ganges and no body would ever know of them."

He liked to know from them if such was a practice of managing train accidents. To that an old villager who was in the age group of above seventy years told him that he had seen so far, four accidents in that area and every time policemen had taken the dead bodies and thrown them in the river Ganges which was hardly fifty kilometers away from there.

"Where are we now what is this place?" Rajesh *wanted to know from the villagers.*

"You are now in between Barh station and Mokama junction which is little over half an hour run from here and Ganges is running parallel to the railway line."

Rajesh felt as if he had fallen from heavens to the earth to know that so many dead bodies would have been thrown in the river Ganges! Obviously to contain the casualty figures which would come to the notice of people of India through media and whose relatives would be eligible for compensation by the Indian Railways. The dead bodies thrown away in the river would be of the persons unknown & unlamented and whose relatives would be searching for them throughout their lives without any result. Though he felt himself extremely fortunate and thankful to God! almighty otherwise his parents and Rajani could have never known, where would have he disappeared while traveling from Varanasi to Kolkata. That day he realized that what would have happened to the elder brother of Rajani whom she has been searching for the last sixteen years and may be possibly she continued with that for her whole life.

Thanks to the Indian Railways, thanks to the police force and thanks to the other rescue & relief teams and of course thanks to the people of the country who took everything whether due to human elements or due to natural factors as something which was lotted, which was fated, which was destined and which was definitely the cruel act of God- the supreme benevolent and the biggest thanks to the governance system which believed in concealing & manipulating the facts & payment of some amount of compensation to the kins of identified deceased ones as the end of their duties and responsibilities.

In the afternoon another train arrived at the accident site, all the passengers were to be taken to Patna and therefrom they could go to Howrah via another route or wherever, they wanted to go. Rajesh and all other passengers who had escaped safely from the accident collected their belongings whatever they could salvage and boarded the train.

He was cursing throughout the relief journey his decision to leave Varanasi where he had got everything what a person could desire in his life, a job of his liking, people loving him and also a love which was his love reciprocated adequately but even still he was not inclined to return back. Reaching Patna gave him a psychological relief, he got down the train, came to a Public call booth, rang Rajani and told her everything that had happened on the way. She was taken aback and was totally shocked. She took some time to get herself composed to reply back the call and then she requested him to come back to Varanasi and restart the life what he had left or could start his own business as he had become proficient in that business but he was not ready to retrace back and assured her to remain always with her,

wherever, he was and in whatever, circumstances
he was.

****

CHAPTER V

The Search Continues

*A*t length he reached Howrah station after a heart breaking journey of two & half days in fully exhausted condition having lost the charm of coming to a new place; only thanking God for saving his life.

On one hand he had repentance of having left Varanasi where he had got something unimagined and on the other hand he was desirous to continue his pursuit to the wealth of happiness. He came out of the Howrah station with his bag hanging on his shoulder and was amazed to see the maddening crowd and a totally unfamiliar humid & pinching environment due to which he was fully drenched with sweat and was finding himself absolutely uncomfortable.

He saw the Howrah bridge, a marvel of engineering standing on the mighty river Hooghly without any support in between, being the sixth biggest cantilever bridge of the world. However, he was surprised to know that river Ganges which was the emancipator of sinners in Varanasi had become river Hooghly in Kolkata.

As advised he came to the Bus stop by enquiring from some people and boarded a city Bus going towards Bura Bazar side. The Bus was so crowded that he felt difficult even to breathe but he had to travel in that and some passenger standing close to him guided him to get down near Bura Bazar post office.

He enquired from some people the address given to him and walking through the crowded narrow lanes and the road having trams running, Buses & taxies plying, pedestrians and man driven strange type of rickshaws moving, he ultimately reached the place where addressee Mukul Barman could be located after a while.

He was owner of a big milk and sweet shop, probably the biggest in the area and had very big business with many men employed there doing different kinds of jobs. Barman happily received him and asked one of the employees to take him to a room where other boys were staying, for accommodating him there as well. He asked Rajesh to be at ease, relax there and next day onwards he could come to shop and join his job. He also told him that other boys who would be staying with him would tell him everything essential for him and also they will help arrange his food & messing etc.

Next day he came to the shop fully ready for the new situation and joined as a sales boy. He was told that since he was in a new situation getting acclimatized to the situation and understanding the new set up needed his priority and also that one day in the week he could avail weekly off, however, if he liked he could work even on that day for which additional payment would be made.

He felt a little difficulty with the local language which was totally new for him but he found the place full of north Indians and also he could find some Maharastrian people which reasonably solved his problem.

He, keeping himself as a layman, coolly and calmly studied every department associated with the business, starting from procurement of inputs, manufacturing of sweets & other items and sales etc and noticed a variety of irregularities which were obviously affecting the earnings and sales, however, he never expressed anything like that to his co-workers and room-mates but on an off day when Barman was available at his residence, he went to him and apprised him of all those things which became the harbinger of improvement in the shop management and checking of pilferage and improvement of quality and sales.

He got himself settled in the new environment within a month's time and liked to make some newer variety of sweets using cow's milk, mishti doi(yoghurt sweetened with coconut jaggery) and other ingredients which was permitted by Barman and in short time they became quite popular.

He used to ring his father periodically giving him the details of his well being & whereabouts and also send money from time to time for the treatment of his mother who continuously requested him to come back home but he continued giving them his assurance of returning back soon but never told his parents anything about Rajani and what all he had experienced during his train journey from Varanasi to Howrah.

Though his quest for the secret wealth of happiness was keeping him ignited but he was feeling pity for himself that he was trying to catch a black cat in a dark room and whatever ray of light had come on his way he had missed that. Nevertheless he always remembered the words of Swamyji whom he had met in a temple to always rely on the advice of heart whenever there was a situation of dilemma, and also that God! never does anything without a purpose and he had satisfied himself the way life was flowing in the waves of time but then how to forget mother, after all mother is mother.

Everywhere, every teaching has recognized the mother not less than the supreme being and his mother had been requesting and calling him back home, then how to disrespect her? He thought and thought and decided to request mother to give him some more time to continue his quest, if he was successful, well & good, otherwise he would say goodbye to his quest and would return back home.

Barman wanted to make him in-charge of the cash counter because of his honesty but he suggested him to refrain from that idea as the same would limit his movements and obviously his vigilance over different activities would disappear.

The life in Bura Bazar area was a very difficult life being all the twenty four hours in crowd, congestion, filth & garbage. Men, animals, mechanized transport, manual transport, carriages, trams and pedestrians all moving together without grudge & grumble but at the same fueling the chaotic situation. However, he was surprised to see that despite all the odds and problems people were happy.

He saw a large number of poor men from Bihar and eastern Uttar Pradesh engaged in pulling man-driven manual rickshaws. These men would be barefoot holding a small bell in their one hand, balancing a yoke on their shoulder and would be running carrying the mounted passengers on the roads and narrow lanes and by-lanes. Strange but true and a truth available only in Kolkata even in twenty first century India.

He would very carefully observe those rickshaw pullers and was astonished to see that those men had no place to stay or accommodation. Their only belonging was a small bag which they would keep in some known wayside small shop. And at the end of their day, on a metallic plate they would take some flour like substance made of roasted gram & barley mixed together called SATTU, make a thin paste of that with water and take that as ready-made food after which spread themselves on a dirty cloth on the side of pavement and sleep there to spend their nights. They would use nearby public toilet and take bath & clean their clothes with the river water gushing through big pipelines along the pavements during morning hours. Probably ninth or tenth wonder of the world which neither he had ever seen or even imagined.

He mentioned that strange observation to his room-mates one day who simply laughed and told him that the things he observed were very common in Kolkata and they further added that all those men who were living like that were saving every paisa of their earning and would be sending that to help their family members residing in some poor village to ensure a reasonable life to their kith & kins.

He was really astonished to learn of that but at once he thought that probably those poor rickshaw pullers were sacrificing themselves for the happiness of their children and near & dear ones and were deriving their happiness from their happiness.

Despite city roads and lanes being full of garbage and other nuisance and plethora of problems, he saw that people found their happiness in that and he also compromised with the situation seeking happiness for himself.

He decided to visit holy sites and historical places on his off days and other places which were unique to Kolkata and found underground Metro to be very convenient to go to the places connected by that mode of transport. Metro was something which neither he had heard of nor seen in his city of Nasik and nearby biggest commercial capital of India, Mumbai. But Metro connection was available only in certain sectors and city bus was still the most popular mode of transport.

He found buses to be over crowded with hardly some space to board them, however, he observed the passengers to be quite accommodative.

One Sunday he went to Dakshineshwar Kali Temple- the world famous place associated with Rama Krishna Paramhans and Swamy Vivekananda. So serene, so beautiful, so tranquil & soothing was the place, situated on the bank of Hooghly-the Ganges in Kolkata.

It was a mesmerizing very great complex, main Kali temple, twelve sets of Lord Shiva temples, and Lord Krishna temple and thousands of people lined up in several queues to have darshan of the goddess. He stood in a line for half an hour and had the darshan of the goddess, followed by darshan of all Shiva temples and then went to the cottage which was the main abode of Paramhansa and mother Sharada (spiritual wife of Rama Krishna Paramhansa). He immediately remembered the great Swamy Vivekananda who had astonished all the delegates assembled in the Parliament of world's Religions held at the Art Institute of Chicago on 11th September, 1893 by addressing them as *Sisters and Brothers* and gave them and to the world the message of his master, and the Indian philosophy to the west.

"Oh! What a great soul of India, what a noble soul of the universal religion and what a great thinker of Hinduism was Swamy Vivekananda. Every Indian feels proud of him and his thoughts are as relevant to-day as they were over a century back."

Reverberating in his thoughts and continuing in the same thought process he took a boat to go to Velur Matt, the hermitage of Paramhansa on the other side of the river.

The hermitage, an elegant structure built on a large area of open green land was full of tranquility, peace inside, peace outside, peace all around with mighty river touching its ramparts with pious waters spreading fragrance of cool breeze and the divine thoughts of Swamy Vivekananda. He felt absolute peace and forgot that there could be some other secret wealth of happiness. He took KHICHARI (a rice preparation) as prasadam which hundreds of others like him were also taking. An ecstasy came to him, he felt a spec of celestial light having entered his mind and then he felt as if Swamy Vivekanand was asking him to forget about worldly quests and work for the elimination of sufferings of have nots and that would be the best repose of happiness. He got himself perplexed and obviously confused and unknowingly swam into the wilderness of thoughts and in the same confused state of mind, he hired a cycle rickshaw and crossing the Howrah bridge unmindfully came to Nimtala ghat, the biggest crematorium of Kolkata on the Strand Road along the bank of river Hooghly.

He was neither able to enjoy the marvel of the Howrah bridge nor the magnificence of the vast river. He saw a temple of Lord Shiva, a small old temple with Lord Hanuman and goddess Parvati(His consort) by the side of Shiva Lingam. He saw the movement of usual life, the cremation i.e. the last song of death and the worship of super god, Mahadeva (Lord Shiva) all going on side by side with the same ease as if there was no difference between life & death and there was nothing like pleasure or pain. He was spell bound to see that strange neighborhood of temple with crematorium but he got reminded that, whatever, he had learnt from the mythology & scriptures was that Lord Shiva though a family person yet was free of all the bondages of pleasures & pains being totally detached and for him happiness was available anywhere whether that was His abode at Mount Kailash in Himalayas or that was a burning ghat or crematorium.

That increased his confusion further, and sunk deep in the ocean of mental conflicts he came back to his residence where company of his room mates helped to divert his attention but, whatever thoughts he had got at Velur Matt had lost their relevance.

In a couple of days he got rid of his mental confusion & regained normalcy and got fully engrossed in his job. But his quest remained kindled in him searching for that secret wealth which could give him happiness while being a normal worldly human being fully discharging his duties and responsibilities in different capacities of his job & also family life.

He maintained his visits to interesting places of Kolkata. He visited Victoria Memorial and Maidan area on one Sunday and was wonder stuck to see such a vast open area in a metropolis like Kolkata which was so thickly populated and full of garbage & rotten roads.

The memorial was really a monument of beauty, elegance and craftsmanship carved in white marble. He had heard of Tajmahal of Agra for its grandeur and beauty and could guess that to be something like the memorial standing in front of him.

It was evening and darkness was falling. In that crowd some one known to him advised him never to stay in that area after nine hours in the night as that area became the den of all forbidden trade activities.

The Kolkattans were known for respecting women but Kolkata was notorious for flesh trade and such activities and any gentleman was supposed to be back home much before certain specified hours from different areas of the city. He heeded the advice, called it a day and came back to his residence, however, having in mind some other rendezvous for the next off day.

He got down from Metro at Hazra Road underground metro station and came out of that.

He was not familiar with the place, but his friends had told him that Shakti Peetham Kali Temple was nearby and he liked to go there.

He took a road and moved on that but quite a long time had elapsed yet there was no sign of any temple. He enquired somebody about that who told him that he was on the wrong side. *Sometimes mistakes are also bliss*, he thought and moved on.

He saw an interesting scene that on the left side of the road on the pavements a large colony of nomadic type of people existed. They had made small-small tents like structures with polythene sheets and had rags of dirty clothes, utensils and other belongings. Men, women and children all clad in dirty rags were busy in their activities. Some had killed some birds and were roasting their flesh, some were busy in eating the flesh and some were just busy in cleaning the utensils or making some handicraft items but one thing was very conspicuous and that was that they were totally unmindful of what all was happening around them and how the people were moving to & fro on the road, and whatever they were doing was that wrong or right? They seemed quite happy with their life of nothingness and enjoying the things in their own way.

He thought that may be such a scene was there on that day only and what all he saw was just like some temporary occurrence. He decided to observe that next Sunday again and surprisingly the same observation was repeated, however, that day on way back he could reach the Kali temple and had the sacred darshan of the mother goddess.

The finding of happiness in nothingness opened another dimension to him and he felt that those who are not having worldly things are free of worries, anxieties and what all happens around them and are happy with whatever they get as two ends meet.

He was continuing with his usual life routine, once a week ringing to his parents and Rajani separately and going out on off days to some place of importance in Kolkata and see life there. On one off day he was moving on the Dumdum road. The locality on both sides of the road presented a blend of old and semi modern buildings but the life was old. As he reached near the DumDum metro station he saw that pavements on both sides of the road were full of vendors; vegetable sellers, meat sellers and household goods sellers but the scene of interest was that live animals & birds were getting slaughtered practically in open in the midst of garbage.

Kolkata has produced a very large number of intellectuals, revolutionaries and social reformers and was also identified as the city of learners & learned, however, every one seemed happy the way things were existing and life was moving fast unchanged, may be for hundreds of years. What was that? Was that not the thing of satisfaction & happiness to continue living like that? His confusion was increasing as his observations were getting richer and richer.

Whereas, he was searching for the secret wealth to happiness, however, he had already found that nothingness was also the source of happiness and living the life the way it exists was also not less than happiness.

In the silence of sleep when poor would be dreaming of treasures & riches; aspirants of chairs would be dreaming of positions of power; those sitting in high chairs would be dreaming of lack of faith by people in them or revolt against them, corrupt would be dreaming of amassing wealth through unscrupulous means and the saintly people would be dreaming of peace & prosperity to all the people of the world. He was dreaming of a secret treasure chest of happiness which was being carried by Rajani and being given to him; which he was not able to hold properly in his hands and the chest dropped down with a thud and every beautiful thing small & tiny kept inside that got spread out & scattered in the dust and he was not able to collect them back. That dream tormented him to weep & curse himself. Scared of such a happening he got up, however, he was surprised to find nothing around him except the usual way of things which he had become used to but the dream had disturbed him and he prayed God! almighty that such a dream remained a false dream only and never happened in reality. The treasure chest of happiness was his ambition which he was searching for to find out and obviously to keep with himself and of course Rajani was his love, the lady love at whose hands he never wished anything undesirable to happen.

Days were passing by, nights were passing by and his mother's request for him to come back home was intensifying but his quest had become a mirage and as he ran from one pillar to another the post was visible at some other distance, in some other direction and every effort to reach that was going in waste thereby increasing his frustration and his confusion too.

****

CHAPTER VI

The Search Ends

*O*ne evening a gentleman came to the shop to purchase some sweets. He looked a typical Bhadralok- a noble person of traditional Bengal culture. He appeared to be in the age group of above fifty five years and was wearing typical Bengali dress of Dhoti & Kurta and was having an elegant golden frame spectacle on his nose. He was clean shaven with a brilliant radiance on his face over which he had a wide forehead with very few whitish hairs left on his head. Though several sales boys were standing on the counter but he came to him and very softly asked for the items that he wanted. Rajesh attended to him with full courtesy, packed nicely the items asked for by him and politely handed him over the packet and requested him to pay the bill at the cash counter.

After a week the same gentleman came to the shop again, approached him for the items and the old story was repeated. He found him coming regularly thrice a week and collecting the stores of his choice.

One day on his recommendation, the gentleman purchased the sweet which had been introduced as a new preparation by him and he became fond of it. This practice continued unabated and unknowingly both of them developed a silent understanding for each other. A couple of months had passed and the gentleman seemed having become affectionate to him.

"I don't think you are a local person. I find you very different in your behavior and also your accent is different." He asked Rajesh one day when very few people were there in the shop.

"You are right Sir, I am from Nasik district in Maharastra state."

"How come you are here in Kolkata?"

"It is my destiny."

He smiled spreading his lips and emitting a mesmerizing glow from his eyes.

"It is only we who make our destiny. I am sanguine you have come here of your own choice as there is no paucity of job opportunity in your area. People from all corners of the country go to Mumbai in search of job and strange that you have come to Kolkata. Any way I am

happy that you have good thought."

The gentleman went away but he left behind a different thought in him that destiny was not something controlled by heavens but it was something where we played the role.

This reminded him that coming to Kolkata was his own decision and nobody else had motivated him or forced him to do so. The observations he had made so far out of various episodes he had seen were his own inferences. He was continuously repenting of his having left Varanasi where he was not having confusing thoughts and was reasonably happy but any way once steps had been taken ahead there was no going back. Let what may be the outcome, but then he remembered that,

"God! never does something without a purpose and He never tells something beforehand,"

and he thought that there must be something why God! has brought him to Kolkata and he left the things to their own course of flow and decided to leave himself to the waves of time & float the way tide of events turned remembering that tide turns at its lowest ebb and the dawn comes when the hour is darkest.

The noble gentleman kept on coming to the shop and availing his services & courtesies, sometimes enquiring about his well being, and if any new preparation had he added to the menu of the shop. Some small- small informations he would occasionally ask about him and had, by now, come to know of his family details and his background etc and was perplexed to find such an educated man from reasonably well to do family had come aimlessly so far off. But then he wondered! No, no, something must be hidden.

Rajesh was periodically sending money to his parents but whenever telecon was there with them, their only anxiety was that he comes back home. One day news came on television that dates of parliamentary elections have been declared and within a day he found that environment of Kolkata was totally transformed.

The happy, peace loving people had got themselves transformed and the city of joy had become the city of processions, slogan shouting and public speeches; most remarkable being that most of the squares were known as MICHHIL PADA(the square of procession) and gradually as the poll dates approached nearer and nearer life became hellish and things became such that there would hardly be some times available to them to relax and take rest.

He was neither interested in all those things nor had any inclination towards such activities, however, he noticed that sales of his shop had increased by leaps & bounds, consequently all the staff of the shop hardly had any time to be away from duty and the supply of milk not being matching they had to resort to imported substitutes. That continued for over five weeks till the polling were over where after the city life gradually regained normalcy.

He had seen the frenzy of elections earlier in his own place but what he observed then was something of madness, something of frenzy, something of life & death and something hysterical where support to one and opposition to another had crossed all the limits of a cultured race which Bengalis otherwise claimed to be. It was good fortune for him that he did not know the local language and consequently even when workers & supporters of different parties were hurling abuses upon each other, he took them as something of exchange of pleasantries.

The coming of the gentleman to the shop had remarkably reduced and mostly he would come much before the sun-set and without any enquiries he would just take his stores and go away. He would also simply wish him, give the items as asked for by him and attend to other customers, but alas! his contact to his parents and Rajani had also got reduced due to briskness of activities.

Elections were over, commotion & bustle of activities had gone off and gradually normal life had come back. He did not worry to know the outcome of polls. The gentleman had begun coming with his usual frequency of visits and also started enquiring certain things about him and his well being. One evening while going back from the shop he called him to come out for a minute and after having come out of the shop he asked him,

"I observed your behavior much different from others

during the past few days when people had their interest in some one or the other in the polls."

"I did not know anybody here and kept myself away from those activities, otherwise also I keep myself away from such things."

"But I have been continuously observing you as if something haunts you. Could you share with me? Being an elderly person possibly I may help you."

"Why not? Definitely. In fact, I got an idea that there is a secret wealth of happiness and in that quest I have reached up to this place but my observations have got me more of confused than getting what I have been looking for."

"OK. I will help you. Next Sunday evening you come to my house, we will go to nearby park and discuss something which may help you."

He gave him his house address & telephone number and also told him, how to reach there and went away. Next Sunday evening Rajesh reached his house as directed to him and he met the gentleman. They exchanged pleasantries and together walked down to the nearby park.

The park was big one having a lake inside and many old & shady trees. A large number of men, women and children were there busy in activities of their liking. Children were playing, young couples sitting in some corners, elderly men and women sitting somewhere on benches and busy in chit-chatting and some middle aged people in shorts & sports shoes walking briskly on oval shaped brick walk-ways. They saw a shady place at a distance where they went together and gentleman asked him to sit on the bench by his side.

Rajesh narrated to him in details his life and adventures so far and also that he was in quest of secret wealth of happiness- a quest which had come to him during a religious discourse at Varanasi and that he had heard about Kolkata being the city of joy, he had come there in his quest. The old man further wanted to know if he had encountered some instances during his search which might have influenced him and given some idea about the happiness.

He narrated to him every bit of his experiences and inferences made out of his visits to different places in Kolkata and also his confusion about the wealth of happiness.

"Ok, I have totally understood your points and also exactly what are you searching for. But remember happiness is within and not without and is a state of realization. Any amount of riches, luxuries and worldly assets and gains can not give you that."

"Then what is that secret wealth which gives happiness?"Asked Rajesh.

"It is an invisible wealth, which you are referring to as secret wealth and it is available within you. In fact no one need search it outside."

"Then, why people are running from pillar to post and are hankering after finding more and more to be happy."

"No doubt, you are partially correct in your observations but remember what did you feel about those have nots whom you saw at the pavements of Hazra Road. Did you not feel that nothingness was also a source of happiness?"

"Yes, I did."

"Did you not feel the sense of happiness at Velur

Mutt and also, did you not find how one could be happy when you visited Shiva temple at Nimtala and observed the relentless flow of life while walking through DumDum road?."

"Yes, I did."

"Did you not observe that those poor rickshaw pullers were seeking their happiness in the happiness of others."

"Yes. I did."

"Then where is the doubt you are having?"

"I feel whatever observations I made were good for certain class of men or for certain situations and for certain set of circumstances but I am a normal man and I want to live my life as a normal worldly man with my parents, wife and children discharging my duties as a normal family man in happiness with them."

"Good! I am very happy that you have got clarity in your mind about what you are, how you want to live with happiness in your life. I will give you experiences of my own life which may guide you to reach what you are searching for."

"So kind of you Sir."

"So, listen carefully. I hale from a very well to do family based at Kolkata-the place and house where you came to meet me. My parents had very high expectations from me and proving to their hopes & desire I liked to do everything possible. I became a general surgeon and joined at Kolkata medical college as a faculty member. Within a couple of years I could earn a good reputation. Somehow I got a desire to earn more & more of money so that I could lead a beautiful and luxurious life. I got a highly paid offer from Dubai and accepted that and despite objections from my parents I went there and joined the same. Three years I remained there serving at a reputed hospital on contract and thereafter I started my own practice. Within a few months I got a roaring practice earning a lot of money. I was remitting a large amount of money to my parents in India hoping that they would have a luxurious life but my mother was not interested in my money, every time I talked to her, she invariably asked me to come back home. I had, by then, become a star attraction in high society and a welcome guest in their functions and gatherings. In one such function I met an English damsel who had come to Dubai as a part of some study team and was conducting studies on Arabian social fabric. Our meeting went on increasing and we developed a good understanding with each other. We started craving for each

other and ultimately we decided to marry. My parents were not happy with my decision but they were helpless and could not stop me from marrying the British lady.

We had a very beautiful and pleasant life. I would be busy in my practice, whereas, she would concentrate in her studies, however, nights would be only for us. A couple of years passed by like this that we got a son which enhanced our happiness & togetherness. Gradually my contacts with my parents also decreased and my mother stopped making requests to me to come back home. Only sometimes she would express her desire to see the grand son! if I could bring him to India for a couple of days.

I was earning a lot of money and everything of luxury which someone could have we had; that one day my wife Jane suggested me to save money for the son and she proposed to have a bank account exclusively in her name. Though that proposal was not having any logical relevance but I thought, how did it matter whether account was in my name or in her name ultimately it will be for us & our son and therefore I agreed. All my earnings started going to her account and only minimum amount would be kept for family expenses. A time span of ten years of our married life had elapsed and our son had grown nicely and was going to a nearby English school. On several occasions

I tried to take my son to India to his grand parents but under some pretext or the other Jane avoided the issue. After a decade of happy conjugal life I noticed some changes in the behavior of my wife and found her giving much less attention to me. Once I had to go to a nearby place to conduct some specialized surgical operation and had to stay there for a couple of days. When I came back I found Jane and my son not present in the house. I waited for them for a couple of days but they did not come back, then I informed the police. After a month police informed me that Jane had gone back to England not to come back to Dubai again.

"Oh, very sad. You had a very bad experience. I hope Jane would have subsequently repented for that."

"No. She never bothered for me. Whenever, I tried to contact her she avoided me. Subsequently she filed a divorce petition."

"Oh! extremely sad. What did you do then?"

"I accepted the divorce and on the advice of my friends I left Dubai and moved to Canada."

"I understand Canada is a very peace loving country, You should have been in Canada, why are you here back."

"That is my destiny which I decided myself and made and I am happy for my act."

"How did you do that?"

"That is again an interesting story. I joined a very reputed hospital in Ottawa in Canada and restarted my life and gradually it started coming on track but I was averse to thinking of marrying again. I preferred my duty in the night hours when patients need more of attention but less of doctors are available in the hospital.

One night I had a very bad experience which changed the entire course of my life. One very old person may be in the age group of nineties was hospitalized for quite sometimes. He was suffering from multiple ailments and that night around two hours in early morning he started sinking. I was attending on him but I could guess that he would not continue for long and he wanted to see his son before dying. I rang to his son at his residence, who got up annoyed and rebuked me for disturbing his sleep. He told me if his father was dying let him die. His father died and his dead body was sent unclaimed for cremation by state. I came to know later that only next day around ten hours forenoon he came to hospital and without any feeling of repentance went back. This episode totally shook me and I got disturbed about my aged parents. One day in a religious discourse I met an Indian Saint who was white from top to toe & would have been an octogenarian whom I narrated about my state of mind who advised me that only the **fragrance of own soil** *could give me solace and peace and asked me to return back to India to join my parents.*

I had already lost my wealth whatever I had earned and the peace of mind was also gone. I rang my mother and told her of my coming back to her. She was extremely pleased to hear that. I came back home and joined them."

Several years have passed ever since. My father is no more but I am happy that I could be with him when he was leaving the world and I did every thing what a son must do. I have joined Rama Krishna Mission and am fully devoted to serving poor people. When a patient is cured I see a bloom on his face & a glow in his eyes and that gives me extreme happiness. Whatever, I am getting is enough and am very happy along with my mother. I firmly believe, if one wants happiness he can get that only in the **fragrance of his own soil** *without craving for worldly gains and other things which only enhance the hunger and many times they enhance that geometrically."*

"I am grateful to you Sir, you have opened my eyes, the darkness before me has vanished and my search is **over**.*"*

****

EPILOGUE

As a child he would feel extremely happy when there was first rain fall after the hot summer. A very pleasing fragrance would emanate from the perched soil as the rain drops fell on it. The whole environment, the whole village, the whole surroundings would be filled with the fragrance, an aroma typical of the soil and that was a fragrance, an aroma which was unmatched, unparalleled. Any scent of Arabia, any lavender of France, any fragrance of the aromatic essential oil or best incense stick would not emit that fragrance what the perched soil would emit when hit by cool raindrops. No sooner that fragrance, that aroma spreads, the peacocks would dance, the nature would dance; there would be melody, the whispering melody of the flute as if the whole surroundings, plants, animals, birds and other creatures would be singing & swinging in tune with nature enjoying and re-radiating aroma of the soil.

He remembered that fragrance was not just the aroma of soil but that was the invigorating elixir heralding a new life sprouting through the soil in the fields, soil in the gardens, soil in the orchard and the soil around his house. His father would immediately prepare for sowing of new seeds & transplanting of saplings; the grape vines already pruned would bring out new leaves & branches and the river Godavari would change its shape & size by transforming itself from a narrow streak of water to a river full to the brim. The sultry heat would have gone, however, occasional humid weather would be there but the pinch of humidity would not trouble much due to the hope that there shall be plenty of fruits in the new crop. He also remembered that fragrance would not be there only once, rather it would be there whenever soil was in the productive mode due to flowering of trees & crops or when the new fruits would be coming out and when the fruits were ripe. The happiness of childhood had gone off his mind as he had grown up and his desires had expanded their horizon.

When the gentleman told him that happiness was there in the fragrance of own soil, he immediately saw in his mind the video clip being played going on reminding him every piece of happiness that he had received from his own soil during his childhood days when butterflies were the fairies, white cranes having come from far off land of Siberia were the prophets of love, peace & prosperity, vegetable plants & vineyard full of fruits were the treasure chests, the water of river Godawari was the elixir of life, his parents were the gods on the earth and his village was the kingdom of God. He also remembered that whenever, he accompanied his father for sowing the seeds, transplanting the saplings, to water the growing plants, for hoeing weeds from the vegetable fields and for tendering & manuring the grape vines, that gave him the happiness of fulfillment. His mother would always tell him some stories when he went to bed and listening to her he would go into sleep feeling that his mother was tendering him, caressing him to grow fast like his vegetable plants. Whenever he saw his parents tired of work he would always think that when he grew up he would take maximum burden so that his parents were relieved off and got enough moments of togetherness, enjoyment & happiness.

He had understood the message contained in the words of the gentleman and obviously his search for the secret treasure of happiness had come to the end. His inner sense and eyes had got the light which had given him the realization that he was searching for something which was already available with him but he could not recognize that. He was thankful to the gentleman but for whom he would have endlessly continued with his search, however, without reaching the goal.

He rang his father and without enquiring anything he told him that his quest was over and he was returning back home. To the utter dismay of Mukul Barman, having expressed his sincerest gratitude to him, he decided to leave Kolkata-the city of joy but for him the city of enlightenment which had given him the freedom from his mental bondages and also the way to happiness.

His mother was extremely happy to find him back home after a long gap of two years of time and within a couple of months she got fully recovered and became hale & hearty again. His father was delighted to find him a transformed person devoting sincerely his time in caring for his parents, fields, vine yard and the vegetable crop and also having left his habit of going to this place or that place. He expressed to his parents that he wanted to run voluntary classes to teach poor children of his village & nearby villages and in due course of time convert his classes into a basic primary school in the name of his mother.

His contact with Rajani had not been there for quite sometimes which had created a deep sense of anxiety to her and over & above that the health condition of Mrs.Sashtri- the foster mother of Rajani was deteriorating day by day very fast and she was apprehensive of something because of the hint given to her by late Sashtri ji. One day she received a ring from Rajesh of his having achieved what he was searching for and of having returned back to his village. She expressing her annoyance and anxiety requested him to come to Varanasi immediately and help her tide over the situation which was there and whatever else may be in store to happen in coming days.

Suddenly his father found him packing his bag for going again somewhere which worried him but he told his mother everything about Rajani &

also told them very clearly that he was going to Varanasi to bring home their would be daughter-in-law requesting his mother to prepare for his ceremonious wedding.

ABOUT THE BOOK

He was in search of something unidentified which took him from one place to another and realization came to him at Varanasi that he was in quest of secret wealth of happiness.

Rajesh Khobragade got his love but that was not the real treasure which could satisfy his quest.

He continued his search at Kolkata where he saw many facets of life with twinkling of happiness, however, one doctor who had undergone some bitter experiences in life while serving abroad showed him the light. The real happiness was available within one self in the fragrance of his own soil.

ABOUT THE AUTHOR

Author is a Doctorate in Chemistry from the University of Allahabad and has spent over thirty five years in serving the Government of India in various capacities.

His writings are the reflections of truth of life which he has derived from the experiences in serving and interacting with the vast array of people of India.

Several books like MANASI, AN ODYSSEY OF ODDS, AND THE BELL RANG, DESTINY IS NOT MY DESTINATION and A CARPET OF WOUNDS have already got published through CREATESPACE.